komninos

Komninos Zervos was born in Richmond, Melbourne, in 1950. He has performed his poetry in discos, comedy venues, literary festivals, and at factories and schools. He now lives in Sydney with Michelle, Maxim and Zanthi.

komninos

University of Queensland Press

First published 1991 by University of Queensland Press
Box 42, St Lucia, Queensland 4067 Australia

Typeset by University of Queensland Press
Printed in Australia by The Book Printer, Victoria

Distributed in the USA and Canada by
International Specialized Book Services, Inc.,
5602 N.E. Hassalo Street, Portland, Oregon 97213-3640

This publication assisted by
the Australia Council, the Australian
Government's arts funding and
advisory body

Cataloguing in Publication Data
National Library of Australia

Komninos.
    Komninos.
    I. Title. (Series: UQP Poetry).

A821.3

ISBN 0 7022 2355 7   *book and cassette*
     0 7022 2280 1   *book only*
     0 7022 2388 3   *audio cassette*

Contents

Foreword

Komninos makes poetry seem easy.

He makes the ancient and difficult craft appear as if he just invented it. He belongs to the world of today.

Poetry for Komninos is to be enthusiastically shared. His poetry is for performance. It is for public enjoyment, for stimulation and reflection, for reassurance, and for new perceptions.

Komninos, the alchemist, creates pure gold from the amalgam of his inner poetry, his rich raspy voice and the expectations of entranced listeners. His performances are dynamic.

This big, bearded man — dressed in black, curly locks down to his shoulders, voice like the bottom of a whisky bottle, looking more anarchist than entertainer — has a gentleness and common touch that belies his appearance. He connects with ordinary people.

His poems speak of the everyday. Of the jangle of inner-city life, of kitchens and nappies and grandmothers, of being Greek, of being Australian, of celebrating living.

His appeal is universal. I watched him work his magic on the Writers' Train tour in western Queensland. I watched him at ease reciting to the tough drinkers in the bars of country pubs. I watched him inspire the big and little kids at country schools, I watched him win over the graziers in the concert halls of country towns. They all loved him and his poetry. He made them all feel involved. He awoke emotions. He made them laugh.

Komninos has taken poetry back to where it started. He is the bard, the storyteller. He uses the richness of language, the power of performance and an empathy with basic humanity to entertain us with stories about ourselves.

Komninos, I suspect, is a Greek word meaning poetry for everyone.

Read his book, listen to his tape, you will know what I mean.

Laurie Muller,
Publisher and Friend

Acknowledgments

Apart from the front cover and family snapshots on pages 27, 37, and 44, all other photographs were taken by Christopher Ellis, and reproduced courtesy of Christopher Ellis Photography.

that's what poetry's all about

high street, kew east

high street/kew east
where i live/it's a busy street/trams/cars/
motor bikes/ambulances/police cars
street sweepers/bikes/cars/trams/
buses/cars/cars/cars/

caaarrssZZZZZZ

caaaaarrsssZZZZZZ

bbbbbiiiikkessZZZZZZ

trrrrraaaaammmSSZZ

across the road there's a park
it's lovely to look at
over the noise of the cars/buses
trams/ambulances/fire engines/
police cars/trams/buses/bikes/
cars/bikes/cars/bikes/cars/
bikescars/bikescars/bikescars/

the other night/
all of a sudden
suddenly
at 8:58/suddenly/there
was silence/silence except
for the sound of the park/
a squeaky seat/a rocking swing/
nighttime music/a certain peace/
a hypnotizing regularity/

saaawinggggggg

saaawingggggggg

saaawingggggggg

caaaaaaarrrrrr

coming/bus/tram/bike/car
ambulance/police car/silence smashed/ambulance/
police car/ambulance/police car/
ambulance/ambulance/ambulance

22/10/84

instructions to a rock and roll
audience on how to appreciate poetry

if you feel like sleeping, sleep,
or chatting at the back of the crowd,
if you feel like snoring, snore,
but please don't snore too loud,
if you feel like dancing, well,
you'll have to go somewhere else,

but,
if you feel like laughing, laugh,
if you feel like shouting, shout,
if you feel like clapping, clap,
that's what poetry's all about.

if you feel the words reach and touch you,
if they slap you in the mouth, not.
if they stroke your emotions softly,
that's what poetry's about.

if you feel the words undress you,
make you see through different eyes,
if you let the words address you,
that's what poetry's all about.
so,
if you feel like whistling, whistle,
if you feel like hooting, hoot,
bending rhyme and rhythm,
that's what poetry's all a-boot.

9/86

workplace poets tour

now i've known artists and muso's too,
actors and poets, a singer or two,
and i've known art critics, journalists and promoters,
government employees and arts administrators,
and i've known sculptors, dancers and fashion designers,
painters and potters and silk screen printers.
and i've known those who go to the opera,
rock concerts, musicals, movies and theatre.

but the greatest art lovers
the greatest art lovers by far
i have found at their job
or in some hotel bar.
people who soak art like a sponge.
who love to hear a poem or song,
who don't give a stuff and sing right along.
who'll clap and jive and beam you a grin,
just when you're ready to throw the towel in.

cos being a poet can be bloody hard work,
most think you're old fashioned,
some think you're a jerk.
so a smile from the crowd
when i'm reading my verse
when i'm doing my job,
hard work in reverse,

makes it all worthwhile,
makes me feel it's been worth it.

cos i've read at schools and prisons
to very captive audiences,
at folk festivals, pubs and community conferences,
i've read in theatres and in the streets,
and on the radio to disco beats,
i've read at jazz clubs and punk clubs
and rock and roll shows.
where i haven't read, nobody goes.

but the greatest art lovers
yes, the greatest art lovers by far
i have found at their jobs
or in some hotel bar.
people who soak art like a sponge,
who just love to hear a poem or song,
who don't give a stuff and just sing right along.
who'll clap and jive and beam you a grin,
just when you're ready to throw the towel in.

cos being a poet is bloody hard work.
most think you're a poof
the others think you're extinct
they all think you're a bludger
and most colour you pink.
but poets have been round for a bloody long time.
yeah. poets were there before radio and t.v.,
poets were there before libraries,
poets were there before industry.
and poets will continue 'til people exist,
to question this life and the wrongs that persist.
and poets will continue to let people know,
what the papers don't tell us,
what the t.v. don't show.
and poets will work hard,
work hard to write verse,
defy prison, torture and authority's curse.
like rendra and hikmet and ritsos and brecht,
write words that their people will never forget.
cos the words that they write don't belong to the poets,
they belong to the world and all the people on it,
every poem, every song, every saga, every sonnet,
comes from the lives of the people of this planet.
and the greatest art lovers,
yes, the greatest art lovers by far,
i have found at their jobs
or in some hotel bar.

cos they seem to know the value of poetry and song,
and they know to whom the poems belong.
the poems are theirs,
no-one can take them away,
just like the poems i'm reading today.

so they smile through their tiredness,
and give you a grin
which says "thank you brother,
please come again."

12/8/86

poetics

let me expound my theory of poetic
these days you have to make your words electric
to sizzle with energy and still be euphonic
to dabble and dribble in dialectic metaphoric
without too much boring didactic rhetoric
to spell out the truth and still have aesthetic
to bend words and change words 'til they're brightly neon-ic
to capture the sounds at speeds supersonic

    to free the words from their traditional prisons
    of books and libraries and academic institutions
    to undress them, expose them to the whole population
    to let them find their own feet in their fight with television
    to hear them booming from radio stations
    to take the words off the page, give them wings, and let
        them fly to new destinations.

let me expound my theory of poetic
these days the words are electric
searching for beauty in things cacophonic
avoiding the misery of moods catatonic
and weird obsessions with things too sardonic
keeping the pace strong and rhythmic
whether or not it's freestyle or lyric
words and ideas forever dynamic

    these days your words have to make you marshmallow
        mushie
    warmly embrace you like the arms of your granny
    take you away on far away journeys
    take you into the depths of your mind and your body
    and then let you down ever so gently
    then shake you around and slap your face firmly
    or make you laugh so much that you piss yourself silly
    feel the razor's edge across the skin of your belly.

let me expound my theory of poetic
these days
your words must be eclectic
must be E-LEC-TRIC.

19/8/87

dripping taps

i hate
the sound
of drip
ing taps
that drip
and drip
the whole
night through
the drip
is driv
ing me
in sane
that con
stant tap
ping in
my brain
that tap
tap tap
tap tap
tap tap
drip drip
drip drip
drip drip,
drip drip
that drip
that drives
me round
the bend
it nev
er nev
er nev
er ends

it drips
all night

and day
time too
there's noth
ing more
that i
can do
to stop
the drip
drip drip
drip drip
how hard
i try
and try
to turn
the knob
and make
it tight
but it
still drips
drip drip
drip drip
all through
the night

drip drip
drip drip
that drip
that hits
on stain
less steel
and pings
and dings
ping ping
ding ding

drip ding
drip ding
tap ping
tap ping
drip ping
drip ping
tap ding
tap ding
bounc ing
off spoons
and forks
and knives
and plates
that need
a wash
ping ping
ding ding
ping ding
ding ping
that drip
it drips
and drips
un til

i'm real
ly sick
of it
and can
not take
no more
of it
and place
un der
the drip
a sponge
and turn
the ping
in to
a thud
thud thud
thud thud
thud thud
thud thud

3/88

the bombay cafe

friday at the bombay cafe
the gourmet talks ballet with his valet
between the pate, the satay and the entree
cliche after cliche after cliche.
the gay valet sips rose
studies the inlay of the parquet walkway
bored with talk of the plie and the coryphee he stares at the
    ashtray
contemplates croquet, payday and broadway

of being faraway in a santa fe cabaret.
the gourmet drinking beaujolais straightens his toupee
bumps the waiter and a tray of souffle ricochets
on the pathway
in the melee the gay valet says he really can't stay
waylaying his parfait he makes for the foyer
the bombe gourmet relays his dismay
but says okay, hey, see you on monday.
the blase valet says 'you may'
and without delay heads for the parkway
to make his getaway
picks up his coupe, a chevy corvette, and speeds up the
    driveway
to the highway and his weekend hideaway, faraway
far from the passe gourmet, per se.
on the freeway mind in disarray, starting to stray
like a mental replay, a teleplay resume,
he sees the hombre in a hallway in monterey
wearing a bouquet and a crochet beret.
he sees the chalet holiday in norway
with the divorcee and her fiance who liked it
    both ways
dressed in a cutaway boucle negligee
foreplay in the bob sleigh, ole!
a risque threeway interplay.
he sees the reggae deejay from zimbabwe
who nay could say neigh to some horseplay
they lay in the hay drinking dubonnet
lame glistened in the midday sunrays.
he sees the kinky calais couturier on the stairway
vibrating bidet, yelling obey! obey!
the attache of the u.s.a. in taipei
resembled hemingway, codename stingray,
who went astray
and one grey may day
was betrayed by the c.i.a., to his dismay
which released a dossier of hearsay on his sexplay.

he sees soiree after soiree after soiree
and curses the day at the sickbay, the random survey
which led to the x-ray, the immunoassay and the doctor's
    communique
for more tests on wednesday, his nerves start to fray
he prays that that day will be his good news day
he prays that that day will not be his doomsday.

at the bombay cafe the gourmet
gets up to pay, and falls against the papier-mache archway.
helped through the doorway into the laneway he sways
he dreams of his heyday as a matinee devotee
he sways in mental decay, a social castaway
empties a throwaway sachet of faberge
the spray leaves a trail from the alleyway to the subway.

far away in a footscray take-away
a modern day protege of rabelais
au fait with roget and wordplay
drinks cafe au lait and surveys the passing array
day after day after day.

3/1/89

dulwich hill

i am not a television screen.
do you know what I mean?
i am not a television screen.
try not to forget.
i am not a television set.
what you give is what you get.
try not to forget.
i am not a television set.
what you give is what you get.
try not to forget.

13

i am not a television set.
i can hear everything you say
when you're chattering away
up the front or at the back
or when you have a giggle attack
or when you try to answer back
in the middle of my act
when i'm speaking to the class
although i'm speaking very fast
my ears are still in tune
and i am present in the room
i'm not a t.v. tube
that you can talk back to
and i know you mean no harm
and i'm trying to keep calm
so i can make you understand
that the attention i demand
is not interrupted by t.v. ads
'cos the short time that we had
meant we had to hurry through
and there were so many things to do
that we didn't have time to stop
for every comment that we got
'cos we had to produce the goods
to put in the carnivale book
so the world would listen to
every single one of you
and what you have to say
through your poems and your plays
and sure we had some fun
and we got some good work done
and we listened to everyone
but we'd only just begun
to understand what it means
when i say
i'm not a t.v. screen

15/6/88

monologues

monologues?
monologues
i'll tell ya about monologues, man
they're like this, man
like this
like listen right
like some people callem soliloquies right soliloquies
sounds pretty silly to me
soliloquy
i like monologues
one person speaking
doing a rave
raving, man
about something they feel strongly about, man
like me, right
i feel strongly about shakespeare
and it shits me when someone says shakespeare sucks
can't stand it when someone slags shakespeare

i chuck a mental
i freak out bad, man
ya know
i freak!

cos this dude
this shakespeare cat
he was cool
a real super smooth cool dude, man
yeah.
a real cool cat
he was smart
he was the smartest, man
he was the smart of the smart
he could outsmart anyone in his day, man
and still have smart left over
man, he was smart
man if i had his smart
if i was as smart as this cat
i'd be the greatest poet in the world
maybe even the southern universe
baaa. baaa.
get it?
he was smart.
he was so smart his brain hurt
from thinking
and writing
his poems and plays
he was smart
he knew about everybody
in his country
in other countries
he knew about everybody
what people do
what people think
what people say
he could make up a good story too, man

it's very important to be able to make up a good story
life depends on good stories
even why you're late for class
hey that's deep
vveeeery deep
but this shakespeare
he was a hero
a legend
he could tell you things about life
about people
about yourself
he was so cool
he was cool to the max
you know what i mean the max
i mean to the end
the furtherest
the most way out of the way out
he was so way out
he was far out man
ya know

i swear
i mean i swear
this cat was cool
believe me

sure
sure!
he spake a funny language
but whataya expect
he never saw no television
he never learnt to talk like miami vice
like rambo
like mick dundee
like kylie minogue
there was no neighbours five hundred years ago, man
no perfect match
no hey hey it's saturday
no comedy company
no
none of that stuff
no radio either
no stereo
not even mono
definitely no videos
no walkmans
nothin like that
not when shakespeare was around
everything was live
in the flesh
person to person
face to face
live
live
live
entertainment
no instant replays
no fast forward through the ads.

remote control
push button
electronic
entertainment
real people
real audiences
no canned laughter
no applause signs
no fake crowd noises
man, this was the real thing
the original
the one and only
the tops
the first and foremost
theatre of life
no re runs
life in the streets
life before the dole
life without push button toilets
life without aids

life without condoms
life as it was
once upon a time and long ago
ugly and beautiful
passionate, man
like your girlfriend's hot kisses in the back of a panel van, man
hot. man.
he was hot
this shakespeare cat

he speaks to you, man
you know what i mean, man?
you know what i mean when i say he speaks to you, man?
he knows about you
he tells you what he knows about others
he SPEAKS to you, man
from 500 years ago he speaks to you man
spoooky
in his plays, man
in the characters of his plays, man
in the monologues of his plays, man
the monologues
the raves
get me?
the monologues
he speaks through his monologues
i mean
        he hath spake to me man
shakespeare ruleth!

20/7/88

audience response

well you strut your stuff
spill your guts
undress yourself
bleed on the stage
and finish
and wait
what do you get?
clap. clap. clap.
hanging out for the clap?
maybe an aahh!
maybe an mmmm . . . !
maybe an oohh!
sometimes silence. dead. pindrop silence.
at other times you start with chatter,
and finish with louder chatter.
sometimes a ha. ha. ha!
and occasionally the big clap.
but what does it mean?
what does it all mean?
well, i'll tell you.

clapping means, the audience is still awake.
some of them liked what they heard
and the others were intimidated into following suit
and clapping.
the aahh! means you've touched the audience
somewhere soft and yukky.
aahh! wasn't that nice.
the mmm . . . usually means that the audience
has realised the poem has finished
just a little too late to clap . . . mmm . . . i should've clapped.
oohh! — look out! you've offended someone's values
someone's intellect
but, at least they're still awake.
silence . . . oh no, they're all asleep

or you've said it all, nothing left to be said, stunned silence
or amazement or not knowing
if they should clap, say oohh! aahh! or mmm . . .
chatter and particularly loud ascending chatter means
people came to dance or sing or to be told how to enjoy
    themselves
— not to hear poetry, not to think
or perhaps you haven't really said anything that can distract
the audience from their talking.
laughing, now that's an unusual response.
did you say something funny
or are your friends just embarrassed for you?

and the big clap
yeah, the big clap.
that's when everyone thinks you've finished.

28/9/85

when i first began

when i first began performing
reading my work in public
sharing my thoughts with people
reciting my poems to audiences
i used to open myself like a book
and i found
pretty soon
that people would
underline parts of me
highlight others
scribble notes in my margins
fold my corners
even take whole pages out of my book
post modernists claimed they knew me better than i knew
    myself

astrologists said they thought so all along
police waited for me to verbal myself
priests listened eagerly to my confessions
psychiatrists scratched at their heads and muttered 'hmmm.'
nurturing types stroked my hair saying 'it'll be alright'
herbalists prescribed tea bags
and
soon i tired
of being flicked through
and quoted from
and preached to
so
i closed my book
and only showed the cover
to those who would judge me
and only read from it
selected text.

17/8/90

nobody calls me a wog, anymore

nobody calls me a wog anymore
i'm respected as an australian
an australian writer
a poet.
but
it didn't just happen
i had to assert myself
as an australian
as an artist
stand up and scream it
point the finger accusingly
thump my fist demandingly
assert my identity

say, 'hey!'
'aus tra li a!'
'look at me!'
'whether you like it or not
i am one of you.'
i give as much as i take
and i've given and taken a lot.
and i'll take as much as i can
and i'll give as much as i've got.

and i said, 'australia, hey!'
'you can call me komninos!'
that's right!
KOMNINOS
K.O.M.N.I.N.O.S.
yes, that's right, it's a greek name
yes, that's right, there's no english translation
yes, that's right, it's my first name
yes, that's right, it is rather unusual
but
that's my name
and i guess, australia, we're stuck with it!
and i said, 'hey, australia'
i'm an ozzie too
. . . just like you
fair dinkum ridgy didge a dinky die true blue
it's a fact of history
there's nothing we can do.

and, australia,
whilst i've still got your attention
i'm a poet
that's right
a poet
i write, i read, i perform, i entertain
i earn my living
by poeting
no. no other job

no. not unemployment benefits
a full-time writer
a poet with a mortgage
and a wife, and kids
and gas bills, and a tax file number
just like you

hey, australia!
we need each other
you need me, and i need you

hey, australia
let's have a beer

and
hey australia
i like you lots
since you stopped calling me
'me wog mate kevin'
and started calling me
'the australian poet, komninos!'

2/10/90

from where I came

childhood in richmond

i remember
my childhood
in the backstreets
of richmond
and the visions
that leave
a lasting
impression
where i lived
in a fish
shop with my
mother and father
and the chips
and the smell
and the grease
and the batter
and the stench
from the garbage
and the thou-
sands of flies
that would gather
to feast on
the shop's
throw aways
in the lane
out the back
where the kids
used to play
and from our
ten by twelve
playground built
over the kitchen
we could see
all the tin
rooftops
of richmond
and pelaco
would flash
in bright red
off and on
the stars
the moon
and the flashing
neon
and all the
factories and
smokestacks that
were nearby
was the sight
you could see
as you looked
to the sky
and the trees
you could see
you could count
on one hand
and the birds
must have
flown off to
some other land
i remember
the fish that
would come by
the truckload
and the cats
in the lane
how they'd feast
on the fishbones
and the scales
of the fishes

how they'd fly
like confetti
and my dad
who'd be covered
from his head
to his toes
and his arms
that would
glisten just
like the fishes
he was cleaning
and gutting
and cutting
the heads off.
and the pubs
that stank
of beer
and of piss
and the drunks
that would stagger
and fall
out at six.
up the hill
they would
swagger to
get some chips
or a cray
if they had
a win
on the races
or some prawns
or oysters
'to take to
the missus'
or some
bread and butter
soaked in

worcestershire sauce
to sober
them up
before their
main course.
and my dad
who left greece
when he was
fifteen
with his hope
his ambitions
and a bag
full of dreams
but spent the
rest of his life
as a slave
to a stove
till his dreams
were all greasy
and his hope
had all gone
and the times
he got mad
and punched the
shit out of drunks
we didn't
know why
but were glad
it wasn't us
and my mum
who would pace
up and down
to the kitchen
taking orders
and trays of
roasters and boilers
and flake n'couta

bream and snapper
to the window
to attract
the eyes of
the buyers
and she carried
the burden
of my father's
bad temper
when the shop
wasn't doing
what it should've
or he was
worried 'bout
the price of
potatoes
and her nerves

were internal
but her anger
was showing
and her legs
would swell up
from all of
that walking
and i often
saw her in
some corner
crying
in the fish shop
in richmond
from where
i came.

1/83

if i was the son of an englishman

if i was the son of an englishman,
i'd really be an aussie,
i could be a high court judge,
or an actor on the telly,
i could be a union boss,
or a co-star with skippy,
i could even be prime-minister,
or comment on the footy.
if i was the son of an englishman,
i'd really be an aussie.

but my father eats salami,
and my mother she wears black,
my last name's papadopoulos,
and my first name's just plain jack.

if i was the son of an englishman,
i'd really be true-blue,
i could drink myself to delirium,
and glorify the spew,
i could desecrate the countryside,
and destroy the kangaroo,
i could joke about the irish,
the greeks, the abo's and the jews.
if i was the son of an englishman,
i'd really be true-blue.

but my father he drinks ouzo,
and my mother she wears black,
my last name's papadopoulos,
and my first name's just plain jack.

if i was the son of an englishman,
i'd really be fair-dinkum,
i'd be seen and not be heard,
i'd be quiet on the tram,
i'd be rowdy at the footy,
and cold to my fellow man,
i'd build four walls around me,
and wouldn't give a damn,
if i was the son of an englishman,
i'd really be fair-dinkum.

but my father eats salami,
and my mother she wears black,
my last name's papadopoulos,
and my first name's really komninos.

6/81

everyone's in love with rita

everyone's in love with rita
she's the market deli girl
everyone's in love with rita
sweet sixteen, life's in a whirl.

all the men they talk to rita
watch her spin and watch her swirl
all the men, in love, with rita
she's the market's favourite girl.

'come and have a coffee, rita,
come to me, my little girl,
come to me.' says sleezy peter
to the bright young deli girl.

always smiling sweetly, rita
long dark hair and baby curls
all the men lust over rita
she's the market deli girl.

butcher boys they say to rita
'come to visit us, my girl'
no-one else could be much sweeter
than the market deli girl.

she's got lovely eyes, has rita
she's the market deli girl
she sells dips and cheese and pita
sweet sixteen, life's in a whirl.

all the men they dream of rita
make a fuss about the girl
she is innocent is rita
coming out into the world.

the market women they watch rita
they all know she's just a girl
they watch the men who ogle rita
the innocent young deli girl.

they see the way men look at rita
remember when, they too, were girls
they can do nothing to protect her
the trusting innocence of the girl.

all the men they eyeball rita
innocent young market girl
as she grows they will mistreat her
as their sexual schemes unfurl.

soon they too will tire of rita
start looking 'round for other girls
'hey! here comes rita's little sister
come! we buy you coffee girl.'

16/2/89

the arrangement

he tells you,
     to smile,
          when you go to goombara's,
and you eat,
     the sweets,
          that she tries to feed you.
and you smile,
     all the while,
          she tries to tell you,
of a cousin,
     of a friend,
          of an uncle of hers.
he tells you,
     to smile,
          when you're washing the dishes
and goombara,
     beside you,
          secretly whispers,
he's got money,
     he's honest,
          he doesn't play horses,
that cousin,
     of a friend,
          of an uncle of hers.
he tells you,
     to smile,
          as you wave them goodbye,

in the back,
     of the holden,
          dad worked hard to buy.
don't forget,
     what she told you,
          about that guy,
the cousin,
     of a friend,
          of an uncle of hers.
he tells you,
     to smile,
          as you're driving home after,
and you listen,
     as mum says,
          you're not getting younger,
and dad says,
     he thinks,
          you couldn't do better,
than the cousin,
     of a friend,
          of an uncle of hers.
so where is,
     the smile,
          as you cry in your bed,
and you think of,
     the things,
          goombara has said,
and the things,
     that you,
          could be instead,
of the wife,
     of a cousin,
          of a friend,
          of an uncle of hers.

                        9.39pm 1/1/83

goombara = friend of family/matchmaker

kastellorizo

my family came, my family came, from kastellorizo
been living in the land of oz, for eighty years or so
they called them refs, they called them wogs, they called them
so and so's
but they survived, the racist jibes, for eighty years you know.
now my papou, he's ninety-two, he watched the family grow
it grew and grew, and grew and grew, the greeks like sex you
know.

*my family came, the cazzies came, from kastellorizo
been living in, the land of oz, for eighty years or so.*

from fish and chips, and steak and eggs, they built their family
homes
on good australian soil they built, they helped australia grow
and in their homes, their souvenirs, from kastellorizo
the hallowed map, the harbour view, the painted plates on show
and photographs, old photographs, that told a tale of woe
of poverty, and tyranny, under the bed they go!

*my family came, the cazzies came, from kastellorizo
been living with, the memories, for eighty years or so.*

their children grew, they went to school, they learnt the aussie
ways
they changed their clothes, they changed their talk, they even
changed their names
but in the house, the parents taught, that cazzies they will stay
a cazzie born, a cazzie be, until their dying day
'cos everything that's greek is good, it's always been that way
and cazzies are, the best of all, my old yiayia would say.

*my family came, the cazzies came, from kastellorizo
been living in, a time-warp zone, for eighty years or so.*

at weddings and, at christenings, they'd sing the cazzie songs
we did the cazzie dances, and we all would sing along
and all the stories, you would hear, about this grecian isle
would put it on, a pedestal, a faultless pure lifestyle

but reality, as time goes by, gets twisted, warped and changed
and the longer, they had been here, the bigger the myth became.

my family came, the cazzies came, from kastellorizo
been living in, the past too long, for eighty years or so.

the myth of kastellorizo, so good, so greek, so great
to live by myth, in a changing world, simply does not equate
'cos no man can, an island be, the proverb wisely states
and progress never comes to those, to those who sit and wait
and so we see, the culture clash, worship of myth creates
you can't live in, another time, another mental state.

my family came, my family stayed, in kastellorizo
been living with the myth too long, for eighty years or so
the cazzies came, the cazzies stayed, in kastellorizo
they left reality behind, some eighty years ago!

25/9/89

under the bed

under the bed
hee hee hee
there was paula
and gail and bev and me
gail's birthday party
other kids had gone home
hundreds and thousands
bread seemed funny to me
anyway
bev and paula and gail and me
were under the bed, see
we were under the bed you see
and we
and we, . . . well we . . .
kissed.

19/6/85

granny's big pink underpants

granny's
big pink underpants
is what i think of
when they ask me to go back
to my earliest memories.
me
under her warm black dress
next to her big pink underpants
elastic round the edges
left railroads
across her soft white/pink skin
skin
that smelt so sweet
so, so soft to touch
lying for hours
cuddling closely
to granny's
big pink underpants.

18/6/85

the perplexities of monogamy

when it was you and me
it was yours and mine and ours.
but
since we have become three
it's you and me and him
and bottle time
and burp time
and cereal time
and solids time
and play time

and nap time
and bath time
and nappy time
and nappy time
and vegetables time
and custard time
and crawling time
and toy time
and songs time
and nursery rhyme time
and games time
and walk time
and hug time
and kisses time
and cuddle time
and peek-a-boo time
and story time
and teeth time
and seda-gel time
and sleep time
and your time with him time
and my time with him time
and our time with him time
and your time alone time
and my time alone time
and his time alone time
and there's not all that much time
for my time with you time
and your time with me time
and time . . .
we used to just call our time.

9.20am 16/5/89

the baby wrap
for maxim

well you hear a little grizzle
and you slowly unwrap
the bundle that is crying
in a heap on your lap
and you unwrap carefully
'cos it could be a trap
it wouldn't be the first time
he's had a mishap

the bundle could let loose
with a bum like a tap
that will spray you with poo
at the drop of a hat
splattering the mustard
on your clothes, on the mat
so you are ever so careful
how you unwrap

the shawl, the blanket,
the sheets you unwrap
the nighties, the singlets
the nappies you unwrap
you unwrap, you unwrap
you unwrap, you unwrap
till he lies there naked
wearing nothing but a cap
do the baby wrap, do the baby wrap
and you get your cotton balls
and you clean up the crap
that has spread down his legs
'round his front, up the back
in every crease, every cranny
every crevice, every crack
and when he's all clean
you begin to wrap

to wrap and wrap
and wrap and wrap
in nappies, in singlets
in nighties you wrap
in sheets, in blankets
in shawls you wrap
you wrap and wrap
and wrap and wrap

do the baby wrap
do the baby wrap
when the grizzly litle chappie
calls for his pappy
to clean up his nappy
which is ever so crappy
better do it snappy
if ya'wanna keep him happy
do the baby wrap
do the baby wrap

and when that little bundle
is ready to nap
you rub him and you burp him
and lie him on your lap
but his feet start to kick
and his arms start to flap
and he goes all red
and his lips start to slap
and you hear that too familiar
rat-tat-tat, tat-tat
and his face starts to smile
and his feet start to clap
o no! the thundering little bundle
has had another crap
and you just know
ya'gunna have to unwrap
unwrap, unwrap, unwrap, unwrap
do the baby wrap!

10/88

42

maxim, my boy

maxim, my boy, go and play with your toys
leave daddy alone, he's busy you know
max don't touch those books, here's a dinosaur, look
max i don't think you should, now just you be good
hey! stop doing that, gee max you're a brat
oh! no! maxie. NO! no you can't have the phone
leave daddy alone, can't you play on your own?
MAX! daddy said no, can't you just go?
max just go away, find something to play
MAX! get out of there, get out of my hair
go play with your car, max you've pushed me too far
MAX! STOP! that coffee is hot. HOT. maxie hot
it's not for you, find something to do
MAX! what did i say? oh. please go away
the ashtray — DON'T TOUCH! max you're getting too much
MAX! get that out of your mouth, look you're making me shout
no max you CAN'T have that, why don't you just scat?
before i get mad, why do you torture your dad?
no. no. that's daddy's pen, here have this one, then
no don't write on the walls, careful you'll fall
no. no. not like that, let go of the cat
max, daddy said no, hey stop biting my toe
max that's daddy's guitar, you'd be better by far
to get out of here, have you no fear?
max let go of that cord, look i know that you're bored
let's get you a drink, you're hungry i think
now sit in your chair, get your hand out of there
i'll just put on your bib, here play with this lid
use your spoon please max, don't you ever relax?
you know you're a chore, don't throw food on the floor
who'll clean up the mess?, well i will i guess
no! don't squirt your poor dad, i know you're not bad
just playful i 'spose, hey let go of my nose
no don't spill your drink, i'll get a sponge from the sink
HEY! PUT DOWN THAT BOWL! oh. no. maxie. no.

now look what you've done, you're pushing me son
well let's clean you up, WATCHOUT for that cup
no! no more maxim, i'm ready to scream
you're finished i suppose, get that muck off your nose
your hands are a disgrace, let me clean up your face
now go and play with your toys, daddy's really annoyed
no max. not the t.v., just let the knobs be
get away from the stove
max. leave. that. alone.
get out of the bin, it's really unclean
it's yuk and it's kak, max put that brush back
you know the toilet's taboo, it's yuk and poo too
max get out of the bowl, max, do what you're told
shit, you're sixteen months old!

4/12/89

iii

coloured neon night

household haiku

wet shirts on hangers
dance arm in arm on the line
wind gently blowing.

the sudsy water
splashing my naked body
reveals my nudity.

stove top battlefield
bread crumbs egg and splattered fat
thickly waits a clean.

advancing daily
the creeping appendage of
the crawling grass weed.

cats stare and meow
trying to attract my eye
when they are hungry.

visitors remind
me of the things i have not
done around the house.

the traffic noises
wake me announcing the start
of a new work day.

the telephone ringing
renews my relationship
with the outside world.

empty mailboxes
keep me waiting and looking
all day for the mail.

mailboxes are only
ever half full of good news
the other half bills.

nestled contentedly
in warm dirt of afternoon
ginger tom cat naps.

oh. sweet smelling weed
whose sticky substance
        conjures
such a sensual state.

a voice from next door
makes me suddenly aware
of my nakedness.

junk mail reminds me
which places not to go
and what not to buy.

nude to the mirror
showered and powdered
and blinds pulled down.

waiting for winter
and log fires in the fireplace
watching winter pass.

my past surrounds me
looks down at me from the walls
stares from all the shelves.

4/4/86

47

the albion

juice freak
paradise
get drunk
keep nice
keep cool
suck piss
that's all
there is
suck more
suck this
fuck off
snakes hiss
fat men
thin men
short men
he men
who can't
say when
too much
too soon
see stars
see moon
gee tars
old tunes
check shirts
beer guts
home made
hair cuts
tee shirts
that smell
love hurts
it's hell
can't get
over it

drink beer
cure it
get drunk
fall down
get up
next round
get lost
get found
head spins
head flips
beer wins
beer wins
beer wins

green room
caffeine
pinball
machines
drink cups
drink heaps
juke box
green cloth
go home
bad dreams
wake up
feel green
wait till
the night
albions
alright
juice freaks
delight.

2/86

48

brunswick street

fresh faced
clean shaved
head face
post hate
razor blade
marat sade
new junk
post punk
pin holed
ear holes
dyed white
rat's bight
plucked brow
do it now

baker's cool
art drool
see you
where the
trendies rule

slick street
pointy feet
razor cut
trendy rut
pre neo
post boho
50's slick
60's schick
70's shit
80's hit
purple pit
jones beach
dry retch
black cat
dirty rat
mental scat
coffee sip
rhumba's hip
see you
on the
arty strip.

8/2/86

49

city haiku

stray dogs in the street
slinking by jaggered brick walls
wet saddened eyes.

cars fart out their fumes
trams roar down the busy streets
commuters commute.

through the concrete footpath
little weed begins to shoot
trampled underfoot.

the buildings turn from
white to grey from grey to black
from black to blacker.

the birds sit perched
on statues and window sills
poles and power lines.

sparrows swoop to scoop
the scraps people leave behind
flying off quickly.

potted plants turning
it seems a duller shade of
public service green.

people push and shove
move to the back of the bus
push and shove and rush.

trams make wires sizzle
as they pass and leave behind
a whistling sky.

a person seated
cross legged chanting mantras
to city rhythms.

the oppressor wears
a suit a collar and tie
and polished shoes.

the oppressed look
as if that is what they are
under the disguise.

the drunk offends
those who find him offensive
leaving others alone.

each face that passes
a poem a short story
a library full.

at the rubbish bin
dressed in op shop rejects
a woman searching.

2/4/86

in the city

in the city cars whizz by you so quickly
and the traffic moves so fast
and the trams and buses and
trucks and trains
and fire engines and tow trucks and
street sweepers and ambulances
and police cars and sirens
and screeching brakes
and beeping horns
and motor bikes
but . . .
in
the
bush
you
can
hear
a
semi
as
it
comes
from
miles
and
miles
away
and
as
it
gets
closer
it gets
louder and
louder and and
louder and closer
and loudest as it
passes
and as it gets further
it gets quieter
and further
and quieter
further
away
until
you
can
hear
it
less
and
less
un
til
it
fades
in
to
the
night
from
which
it
came.

nuclear dreaming

black coffee nights
all night
black coffee nicotine nights
nights of nicotine and black coffee
toss and turn nights
caffeine nicotine bad dream nights
no sleep creased sheet nights
green leaf smoke heaps nights
throat sore nights
smoke more nights
sing blues nights
blues, all night through, nights
caffeine
nicotine
bad dream
blue and green nights

coloured neon night
shines bright
neon light lights the night
sky is bright with
neon
neon
neon
ne-on
ne-on
ne-on
and on
and on
and on
and on
into the night
the black coffee
hard drug rock music night
beer swilled guts filled night
beer soaked cheap thrill night

loud noise night
girls/boys night
street wise night
red eyes night
the red yellow and flashing blue night
flashing blue light
flashing blue light
the multicoloured
kaleidoscope night
cacophonic neon night
catatonic coffee night
black coffee night
black coffee nights
black coffee nights

17/4/86

the country

when a city kid
goes to the country
the ants don't roar like a tram
the birds don't scream like sirens
the trees don't smell like a tip
the rivers don't flow like the traffic
the animals don't live in a zoo
the people don't box themselves in
the cops don't smell like pigs do
the people don't forget that they're people

when a city kid goes to the country
the impressions don't hit him like a motor car accident.

22/3/86

55

bustalk

oh! i know!
i knoww!
y'know. i know
oh. no! i know
yes. i know.
ya'know?
i knowww!

ohh! i knew!
of course i knew.
i knew you knew too
and i knew you knew i knew.
ohh! i knew!
ay! what ya say?
i say. what ya say?
i can't hear.
in this ear
this ear 'ere
it don't hear.
what ya say? ay!

i saiiid.
she said i said she said
but i never said what she said i said.
but she said i said what i said
what do 'ya say?
i ask ya.
not that i'm asking you.
i'm just saying.
whataya say?

see?
see what i mean?
what can ya say, see.
ya see what i'm trying to say?
well, i mean.

ya see what i mean?
i mean what i'm trying to say is
things are not what they seem

things are not what they seem, see.
the thing is, things are not
what they seem.
i dunno!
sometimes i just dunno.
ya know?
i don't know sometimes i just don't know
oh! i mean i know.
i knowww!
ya'know?
i know.
anyway,
that's another story,
here's me stop love,
nice talkin' to you.
bye.

now, don't you say nothin' about what we been talkin' about
ya hear.

6/87

57

past convictions

silver top t2618

i gave away my car
to get away from the fascists
the parking fines
the breathalyser tests
the random checks
and roadworthies
registration and insurance.
but it seems
you can't get away from them
that easily.

hailed a cab
the other night,
just left some friends
feeling pretty mellow
"can you take me to footscray mate?" i said
"Sure" he said, *"footscray, i like footscray,
i come from altona, dat's my erea."*
he drives on. then he says
"just finished work eh!"
"no, visiting friends."
"which part of footscray?"
"gordon st." i said
"oh the commission flats."
"no, that's an elderly citizens home"
"oh the boarding house, opposite essex st."
"no, not the boarding house"
*"maybe you want to check to see if you've got enough money
to get to footscray"* he says
as he slows the cab down.
"look mate, when i get in a cab
i know how much money i've got in my pocket.
when i get a cab i know how much it costs,"
and in greek say "prohora"
— get going

"you greek?" he says.
"no, you are" i say.
"so just do your job and drive me to footscray
because you've already insulted me enough
by your inferences and attitudes."
"what you mean, why you get so upset
if you like i drop you at city rank — get another cab."
"and pay another flagfall."
"no, i'll take the flagfall off,
what's a dollar, anyway. i don't care about dollars.
1000's yes but a dollar."
"just drive will you,"
he drives.
i boil.
he says "my daughter is going to greece soon.
she's in the police force."
i look out the window.
"where did you say you wanted to go?" he said,
"the boarding house in gordon st.?"
"look! you said, that's where i'm going,
i'll tell you where i want to go when we get there,
just drive.
don't talk."
we drive down hopkins st.
"drop me at the pizza shop"
i didn't want him to see where i lived.
he stopped.
i paid him.
and as i closed the door,
said "sorry, if i've dirtied your taxi."
and as i looked back,
found him checking to see if i had.

superwog

look!
up in the sky.
it's a bird.
it's a plane.
no . . .
it's SUPERWOG.
strange visitor from a european country
with powers and abilities far beyond those
of normal anglo-saxons.
who can gut and fillet mighty man-eaters,
pick up hot dim-sims in his bare hands.

faster than a squirt of vinegar,
more powerful than tsatsiki,
able to use the lifts in tall buildings.

and who,
disguised as con pappas,
mild mannered fish monger
at a great metropolitan shopping complex

fights a never ending battle
against macdonalds,
kentucky fried chicken,
and the american take away.

8/84

wilhelm reich's mass psychology of fascism

sun,
hot sun
a book
a brilliant blue sky
reich's mass psychology of fascism
cigarettes
a cup of coffee
a mattress
a pillow
body
naked
to the sun
music
soft and greek
peace
shattered suddenly
cops
two
blue eyed, blond haired boys in blue
guns
what's happening?
warrant
get up
get dressed
come inside
cops
two more
front door
what's fucking happening?
you know
let's see your arms
my arms?
what's in there?
my room
o.k. come clean

tell us everything
i don't know anything
well we'll tear this place apart
tear
rip
search
empty
what's this?
you tell me
and these seeds?
well?
you know what they are
you gonna talk?
about what?
like to have a puff do you?
sometimes
come on tell us everything
what?
don't light that cigarette
why
i'm talking to you — that's why
oh
what's this all about?
got enemies have you?
what do you mean?
well someone's put you in
had any fights lately?
my lifestyle seems to attract enemies
what does that mean?
well i'm a non-conformist
don't do what other people do
upset people if you're not the same as them
i guess
where do you work?
youth worker, richmond
you have to conform there don't you?
well i suppose.

well you must have an enemy somewhere
i can't think of who.
write poetry do you?
very perceptive.
**we might be perceptive of something else if we look hard
enough**
anyway do you like it?
what? oh the poetry, it's alright
tear
rip
clink
empty
look at
read
pry
snigger
stare
throw
mess
stomp on memories
trample feelings
finding nothing
past convictions?
no
this will be your first, eh?
if you take it to court
what makes you think we won't?
well, i'm not exactly a menace to society
and really what have you found?
a few seeds and a bit of stuff
well boy you must have some enemies somewhere?
have you had any heroin lately?
do you still beat your wife?
well son what are we going to do with you?
you tell me.
well you can think yourself lucky
lucky, why?
we won't take you to the station this time.

they left
i, still
trembling,
sat and smoked another cigarette
put all my things back in my drawers
picked everything up
found some dope that they had missed
smoked it
took my clothes off
put a record on, soft and greek
sat in the sun
a cup of coffee
a brilliant blue sky
looking at the book
wilhelm reich's mass psychology of fascism
and thought
how lucky
that i'd already read it.

28/12/83

paranoid?

paranoid?
who said i was paranoid?
i'm not paranoid?
paranoid?
who me?
high court judges say
telephone tapping's o.k.
i.d. cards are on the way
operation noah, the drug offensive, breathalyser tests
car searches, street searches, and all the rest.
who said i was paranoid?
cigarettes rot my lungs each day
whiskey causes liver decay

drugs blow brain cells away
social diseases are a constant threat
staying alive's just staying out of debt
paranoid?
who said i was paranoid?
heroin, a.i.d.s., unsafe sex
test tube babies and wet chex
genetic engineering will be next
apartheid, gunsquads, laser tatoos
helicopters, helicopters, coming down on you.
paranoid,
who said i was paranoid?
cops carry guns on their beats
cameras on the buildings and in the streets
police are taught to suspect everyone they meet
a.s.i.o. men at demos look so conspicuous
you can tell them by their haircuts and the way they dress
paranoid?
who said i was paranoid?
i'm not paranoid!
paranoid?
who me?

hopkins street hustling

the smell has gone from hopkins street
the air has cleared, a little bit,
the stench of dying bodies,
the gaze of empty eyes,
the sight of broken lives,
the keepers and the kept,
the users and the used,
downtrodden and abused,
no longer walk these streets,
in search of their next fix,

their dealer for to meet.
no longer sip long blacks,
whilst scratching at their tracks,
no longer wait in cars,
or market coffee bars.
no longer make that deal,
the money for the foil,
no longer make that dash
to the market with their stash,
and their coke can and syringe,
for their next narcotic binge,
no longer nod to sleep,
in the mall or in the street.
no longer fall about,
on the station, quite spaced out.

the smell has gone from hopkins street
the boys in blue are on the beat,
yeah. they really put on the heat,
searching people in the street,
stopping cars and taking names,
it only took a week.
now,
all is quiet on hopkins street.
but,
the boys and girls in blue,
just move the problem on,
who knows where this action's gone.
for those who were watching,
we just caught a glimpse,
of the lives of the addicts
and how ugly that is.
now they've gone somewhere else,
to where other people live,
and they've left us,
with the smell of our own lives again.

24/3/87

69

if god exists

if god exists,
let him produce
a black female jesus
from the side of a man's head.

and when the black female jesus
was fully grown,
she killed her father.

unfortunately god
doesn't exist.
but i do.
and i've got this black female jesus
growing out of the side
of my head.
it might be a pimple.
i'll ask the naturopath
before thursday.
if thursday doesn't
ask the naturopath
before me.

it's great to be mates with a koori

it's great to be mates with a koori
to know a gay man or two.
to have five lesbians for dinner,
and to cook them a vegetable stew.

it's a-m-a-z-i-n-g to have your chart done,
consult the tarot and the i ching.
to have a therapeutic massage,
and give the naturopath a ring.

it's sound to be found at a rally,
waving banners and shouting abuse,
at the c.i.a.'s involvement,
in wars and military coups.

it's hip to sip coffee at rhumba's,
whilst having an artistic chat.
drink pots and pots
of earl grey,
at baker's or the black cat.

it's grouse to pronounce spanakopita,
the way the greek people do.
make humus at home in the blender,
tsatsiki and babaganouge.

it's great to relate as a person,
and not as a woman or man.
how dare you assume i'm heterosexual,
and hug friends as hard as you can.

but who do you see in the mirror,
when there's only yourself and you.
and who really knows the truth,
of the fascist, that lives inside, you.

once

once,
i thought i was a lesbian.
i was convinced i was a lesbian.
i had started to question all the double standards,
and began to dislike men.
in fact,
i began to hate men.

i really despised men.
i began to hate myself for being a man.
i began to feel guilty about being a man.
i felt guilty for all the men.
i felt the guilt of 1000s of years.
i felt guilty when going to bed with women,
i felt guilty about being a man.
so, in my mind
i became a lesbian.
so that i could save myself from going mad,
so that i could understand women more,
so that i could understand men more,
so that i could understand myself more,
and to not feel so guilty about going to bed with women.
'cos it was alright for lesbians to go to bed with women,
and to dislike men at the same time.
and,
if you think that's pretty weird,
you should hear about the time i thought i was a bisexual
hermaphrodite,
i really fucked myself up, then.

life's really tough for an aware together polymorphous
perverse polygamous heterosexual male these days.

                                                    10/86

i hate caars

i hate caaaaaaaaaaaaaaaaaaaaaaaars
they tell what people are
if they're rich or if they're poor
who's got less and who's got more
such a privileged possession
for a globe that's in recession

72

such a waste of good resources
we could use for better causes
such a selfish luxury item
drivers have no-one beside'm
as they drive to work alone
and at night from work to home
'cos this is a capitalist de-mocracy
one person — one car you see.

i hate caaaaaaaaaaaaaaaaaaaaaaaars
they leave my peace with scars
they bother me at night
and wake me with a fright
they fart out their foul fumes
i can smell them in my room
when i open the window and door
i can hear their constant roar
it's driving me insane
the pounding in my brain
from morning to day's end
it never, never ends
that persistent rumbling drone
everywhere i rrrrroamm
rrrrrrrrrrrrrrooaaaammm
rrrrrrrrrrrrrrooaaaammm
rrrrrrrrrrrrrooaaaammm
rrrrrrrrrrrrrooaaaammm
rrrrrrrrrrrrrooaaaammm
i hate caaaaaaaaaaaaaaaaaaaaaaaars
for the power symbols that they are
young boys trying to impress
to prove that they're the best
fat tyres, v.8.s, extractors
guzzling petrol by the litre
their tender teenage years
spent on brake and clutch and gears
dragging others at the lights

a reckless regard for life
a mindless display of power
at a hundred Ks an hour
drive to nowhere proving nothing
just to show they're really something.

i hate caaaaaaaaaaaaaaaaaaaaaaaars
mix disastrously with bars
for those who've had a few drinks
they won't stop to think
of the danger to their lives
and far too many die
in death traps and in heaps
that cost so much to keep
balding tyres and worn out treads
better catch a bus instead
faulty steering, faulty brakes
a few beers that's all it takes
why should you take that risk
catch a cab if you're too pissed.

3/12/87

i'm convinced that a.i.d.s. is a c.i.a. plot

i'm convinced that a.i.d.s. is a c.i.a. plot,
conceived in some germ warfare laboratory
deep in the heart of Texas
developed to combat the impending
danger of the sexual revolution
the revolution that bombs can't touch
that guns won't shoot
that police can not arrest
that up till now
could not be stopped.

the neutron bomb
the latest advance in population control
leaves buildings standing
whilst blowing people away
clean
clean up all the dissidents in fitzroy in one clean hit.
whilst preserving the unique architectural styles
as prescribed by the national trust
a renovator's dream
red hot specials
mandatory "cool off" period applies
fitzroy for vacant possession
very clean
but, some time required for the investment
the red hot special,
to realise its full potential,

the a.i.d.s. bomb
the newest advance in population control
even better than the neutron bomb
gets all the gays straight off
then the lesbians
then the feminists
and eventually the leftists.
slowly
but surely
the a.i.d.s. bomb will kill all the dissidents
of fitzroy
leaving the architectural features intact.
and instantly re-saleable or re-rentable

no, you're just paranoid
you'll say.
it will never spread so far,
gays will stop doing what they do.
feminists and leftists
won't have anything to do with them

in fact,
no-one will have anything to do with gays
jokes will be aimed at them
they will become the new scum of society
we'll all have someone lower than
us to kick.
we'll all be safe at home
we'll all be the good little people

i'm convinced that a.i.d.s. is a c.i.a. plot.

18/12/84

the tanks rolled through the streets

the tanks rolled through the streets,
          i was worrying about guest lists,
the crowds that gathered outside were all dispersed,
          the bridesmaids' dresses were white with red stripes,
those who remained,
inside the polytechnic,
were hungry, were cold and needing inspiration,
          the bombonieres were our design,
          with matching placecards,
          and invitations,
for three days they were calling for,
bread,
education
and freedom,
they were singing 'pote tha yine xastouria',
they screamed down with the hunta,
down with papadopoulos,
out with american bases,
they broadcast messages to the nation,
urging people to support them,

to defy the curfew,
to take to the streets,
> we married at st. constantines and helens,
> photos,
> in the alexandra gardens and then the reception,
> they served,
> a seafood cocktail,
> a crumbed whiting entree,
> and a choice of chicken or beef,
> we presented our speeches,
> did our dances,
> and had bomb alaska for sweets.

the tanks rolled into athens on the third night,

> they all said the bride looked lovely in white,

the students were going to be taught a lesson,
> we were carried at the head of the wedding procession,

they stormed the buildings,
broke through the gates,
armour firing,
in the dark of night,
students screaming,
taking flight,
not many remained,
not many survived,
the protest was over,
their blood had been shed,
> we were driven to the hotel,
> booked into the bridal suite,
> opened the champagne,
> our wedding night
> we now had a licence,
> everything was alright,
> only we had remained,
> we turned out the light,
> the virgin's blood,
> had stained the bed,

the massacre in 1973 heralded the end of a military dictatorship
    in greece
the marriage in 1973 heralded the beginning of a new one in
    kew,
chile, el salvador, poland, afghanistan, the philippines,
    end all dictatorial regimes,
mt. waverley, sunshine, prahran, abbotsford, and preston,
end all dictatorial regimes.

7/83

fringe network anthology

on this day
11th of november
1918
the world
celebrated peace
after the war
to end all wars.
on this day,
11th november
1936
my father
arrived from greece,
and as he descended the gangplank
all australia stood still . . . or so he said.
on this day,
11th of november
1975
i took off my white coat
locked the laboratory
did not sign the sign-out book
at kraft foods ltd.
and sped to join 100,000 protesters

yelling general strike
at the gates of government house.
on this day
in 1975
the trade union leader
said
go back to work
we will go to the polls
we live in a democracy.
on this day,
11th of november
1984
the self proclaimed fringe
reads poetry
in the park
just a rifle shot
from the gates of government house.
there were other wars
my father lived and died unnoticed
the election was lost
the trade union leader became
        prime minister
and one day, the poets will be carted off to the m.c.g.

                                        11/11/84

my friends

my friends
get drunk at cheap hotel
after cheap hotel
day after day after day
and return home with wilted vegetables
and aching heads and guilty consciences.
my friends
take fast train trips to fitzroy street
to score
get on
and get off again some time later.
my friends
sit in coffee lounges

learning to say spanakopita and macchiato
spending their present
contemplating their future and their past.
my friends
design pamphlets
mix glue
and spend their nights plastering the walls of popular streets.
my friends
write songs
write poetry
paint pictures
make films
act roles
dance wildly
express vividly.
my friends
sit wide eyed mulled up
bonged out
in front of television screens
night after night after night.
my friends
drink coffee smoke cigarettes
drive motor cars bite fingernails
write poetry to the demon god war.
my friends
were born after the year zero
the year hiroshima burnt
the year man proved there was no god.
my friends
grew up with television sets as baby sitters
suckled by advertising and disney cartoons.
my friends
hailed the beatles as the new messiahs
and rock and roll as a new religion
only to be exploited by their church.

my friends
danced the mekong delta boogie
and the tet offensive rock.
my friends
thought they were living in england until 1972
and knew definitely they were living in the u.s.a. in 1975.
my friends
hold placards march for peace the city streets
in government monitored demonstrations
knowing that the powerful
will not give up that power without a fight.
my friends
did not leave the city in the seventies
who stayed
and who stewed in it.
my friends
have not settled down to a volvo a pool
a home and a family.
my friends
have begun an unending process of questioning
which constantly uncovers the contradictions
of this existence.
my friends
sit at home
crying alone
lonely
in their chosen aloneness.
my friends
sometimes dream of a volvo a pool
a home and a family
or a mudbrick cottage in the bush.
my friends
wilfully lie bi-weekly for their survival
to government counter staff
who know they are lying
and wouldn't help them if they weren't.

my friends
justify their existence
by means of submission to government authorities
conforming to guidelines rather than ideals.
my friends
wash dishes sell coffee
wait on tables pull weeds
do anything to supplement their meagre incomes.
my friends
desperately try to resolve their differences with parents
trying to understand why they spend the rest of their lives
sorting out what happened to them in their childhoods.
my friends
have babies with asians and africans
so that they can have amazing little children.
my friends
want to be parents
before they are too old
to enjoy parenthood.
my friends
resisted the societal pressure to marry
but cannot deny the biological pressure to reproduce.
my friends
think more seriously about parenthood
with each successive abortion.
my friends
fall in and out of love
depending on how insecure they're feeling at the time.
my friends
steal vegetables from market stalls
to help stretch the weekly budget.
my friends
grow their own vegetables
to cut the cost of living.

my friends
take toilet paper from coffee lounges
government buildings hotels and picture theatres
to help cut the cost of shitting.
my friends
are attracted by youth
but know they are beyond it.
my friends
take trips outback
to be closer to the real australians.
my friends
return
knowing they will never belong there.
my friends
learn spanish
so that they can be closer to the struggle in el salvador.
my friends
wake up in strangers beds
with large hangovers.
my friends
count wrinkles and grey hairs on birthdays.
my friends
wait patiently for the phone to ring
or the door to knock or the postman to call.
my friends
work 9 to 5 jobs to afford their social drug addictions
alcohol marijuana coffee and nicotine.
my friends
know what herbs are good for you
and what teabags to drink.
my friends
ask for free range eggs at hamburger joints
to make a political point.
my friends
lick plates in restaurants
to constantly remind the others that people are still starving.

my friends
work hard at being non-sexist
whilst trying not to hate men.
my friends
feed cats kangaroo meat
so they won't eat the native birds.
my friends
have seen mountains grow out of molehills
mount collins place mount nauru and mount grollo rialto.
my friends
have been mesmerised by the fluorescent
lulled by the white noise dazed by the neon
subdued by the transistor and the silicon
and intimidated by the air conditioning.
my friends
and me.

1/87

An audio cassette specially chosen and performed by Komninos and produced by UQP is also available. It Includes:

• high street, kew east •

• childhood in richmond •

• if i was the son of an englishman •

• bustalk •

• dripping taps •

• granny's big pink underpants •

• in the city •

• the baby wrap •

• superwog •

• nuclear dreaming •

• it's great to be mates with a koori •

• the tanks rolled through the streets •

• fringe network anthology •

• mass psychology of fascism •

• the bombay cafe •

• my friends •